manual ······

CONNECTING
Mum
entrepreneurs

It's not **HOW,**
IT'S **WHO!**

Sally A. Curtis
business mums solutions

Published 2015

Publisher: Sally A Curtis - Business Mums Solutions

Graphic Design & Layout: Mélissa Caron – go-Enki.com
Editor: Richard Burian – Richard-Burian.com

Business Development/Growth, Lead Generation, Entrepreneurship, Women's

ISBN: 978-0-9944274-1-0

TABLE OF CONTENTS

YOUR *Goals*

IDENTIFYING YOUR GOALS

There are several parts to building up a valuable business network. These parts will be introduced in the following sections and elaborated throughout the book. Before anything else, you need to know exactly where you want to put your focus.

> **!** **Read the introduction section 'Building and Marketing Your Business'**
> See page 12 of your *Connecting Mum Entrepreneurs* book for the complete text about this topic.

What products or services do I want to offer?

....

....

....

....

....

....

....

....

Knowing what you have to offer is not enough; you must have a vision in order to know where to go next and where to invest your time.

What goals do I want to achieve within the next year with my business?

Identifying who might be interested in investing in your services and products is primordial. By knowing who you want to target, you can discover how to reach them as well and what you can do to appeal to them.

Who are the type of clients who could be interested in my services and products?

❏ Women	❏ Men	❏ Kids
❏ Age 0-2	❏ Highly educated	❏ Likes prestige
❏ Age 2-5	❏ Senior management	❏ Sporty
❏ Age 6-10	❏ Carefree and spiritual	❏ Academic
❏ Age 11-15	❏ Mums	❏ Gamer
❏ Age 16-18	❏ Stay-at-home mums	❏ Fashion focus
❏ Age 20-30	❏ Love technology	❏ Trend focus
❏ Age 30-40	❏ Health focussed	❏ Social
❏ Age 40-55	❏ Business owners	❏ Reserve
❏ Age 55+	❏ Unemployed	❏ Business owners
❏ Single	❏ Married	❏ Concerned about image

Others: ....

....

....

....

....

....

....

As in any other area of your life, being in business brings up a lot of challenges and fears that you will need to overcome; but fears and concerns can also be part of your own perception only. The key is not always to eliminate all your fears and concerns but finding a balance to help you to manage your day-to-day life and match it with your business goals seamlessly.

What concerns do I currently have?

❏ Feeling overwhelmed

❏ Too much to do

❏ Fear of failing

❏ No reputation

❏ Knowing what is working

❏ Eliminating all issues outside of my control

❏ No one to help

❏ Prioritising time

❏ Prioritising tasks

❏ Prioritising revenue needs

❏ Knowing what isn't working

❏ What actually creates my revenue/profit now?

Other concerns:

....

....

....

....

....

....

....

....

For every concern we have, we will know someone who has succeeded doing the opposite. Everything doesn't need to be perfect but your attitude and mindset does!

Who can you think of that has broken the mold of your concerns? What did they do?
It could be a friend, a sports star, celebrity or someone you admired in the past. Our success and strategies can be modelled from other people's successes and made our own.

PERSON	CONCERN	WHAT THEY DID

PERSON	CONCERN	WHAT THEY DID
....	....	....
	....	....
	....	....
	....	....
....	....	....
	....	....
	....	....
	....	....
....	....	....
	....	....
	....	....
	....	....
....	....	....
	....	....
	....	....
	....	....

IDENTIFYING YOUR STRENGTHS

To increase the positive impact you have on people with every interaction you experience, which results in a dramatic rise in your reputation.

'Reputations take a lifetime to build but seconds to destroy'

Simply write down the first three words that come to mind for each question.

What are the qualities in other people that you admire most?

....

What are your unique abilities or talents? What makes you special?

....

Who are your heroes or heroines, alive or present, in myth, legend, religion or history?

....

What are you continually sharing or explaining to your clients and friends?

....

What do they come back for more of or what are they looking for?

....

What do people currently know ABOUT you, <u>before</u> they meet you?
Good, bad and ugly!

....

....

....

....

....

....

....

What is it you <u>are</u> known for?

....

....

....

....

....

....

....

....

What is it you <u>want</u> to be known for?

....

....

....

....

....

....

....

Can others explain you easily? What are they likely to say?

....

....

....

....

....

....

....

....

Have people been INSPIRED to share you with others?
What has occurred? Why did they feel inspired?

What do you want people to now know ABOUT you, before they meet you?
Consider different words or more dynamic phrases or sentences you want people to now say and know about you.

CHANGING PERCEPTIONS

There are many ways to change the perception of others towards you but also your own. Reputation Builders are easy ways to work around perceptions that may stick to you because of your previous work, network, training or simply because people don't know enough about you.

Choose 3 Reputation Builders from the list, or create your own, and write ways you can develop and bring this quality into your reputation of your business / profession. List specific action steps you can integrate right now.

❏ Write a book

❏ Write articles

❏ Public speaking

❏ Specialised skills sets

❏ Share a vulnerable story

❏ Share a story with a few friends

❏ Great customer service or anything that makes you stand out from the crowd

❏ Share a great article that's relevant to the other person

❏ Be a cheerleader for someone else or their cause

❏ Smile a lot

❏ Get in the media / press releases

❏ Give away high value content

❏ Unique experiences

❏ Awards

❏ Share and suggest connections

❏ Success stories: case studies that you can build a great story around

❏ Create a VIP event and invite customers and connections

❏ Leverage off better quality people in network

REPUTATION BUILDER → **ACTION STEPS**

....

....

REPUTATION BUILDER → **ACTION STEPS**

....

....

REPUTATION BUILDER → **ACTION STEPS**

....

....

BUILDING AND MARKETING YOUR BUSINESS

While you are learning and training in your business, the key component is to uncover hidden opportunities. Most of these key opportunities have been there for a long time, but as you have not studied and understood how your networks fit together they were not immediately obvious.

At this stage we are not looking at placing key players in your business, we are looking at defining and identifying your current network. Since most adults have a network with more than 500 people, we want to write down different groups of people rather than individual names at this stage.

What events do you attend?
What Groups, Associations, Memberships and Clubs are you a member of? They can be business related as well as non-business related.

What education do you receive as it relates to your business?

What events can I participate in to reach my ideal clients?

To help you answer this question, think of where (what businesses) your clients go to before and after they use your services. Then find out where these types of businesses network. List as many events as possible, including the ones outside your comfort zone.

Who are the prominent leaders in your life and industry?
It can be mentors or any others.

....

....

....

....

....

Who are you regular business partners, project partners, sounding boards?

....

....

....

....

Who are the best educators you know or have been trained by?

....

....

....

....

....

EVENTS AND OPPORTUNITIES

The business development phase is done using three different mediums: face-to-face, phone or virtual. Our confidence grows dramatically when we understand who we are, what we have so close at hand and how many opportunities are available to us.

As a mum in business, we already have access to a lot of people, we often just don't know how to approach them or incorporate them successfully into our business.

Tips for attending networking face-to-face events:

1. Be confident.
2. Know why you are there and who the types of people you would like to meet are.
3. Ask the organiser or a really friendly person you meet on the way in to point you in the right direction.
4. Once you have done this a few times you will notice other people on the outskirts that are a little nervous. Make them feel comfortable by saying hello and bringing them into a conversation.
5. Practise, practise and practise answering confidently, 'What do you do?'
6. Remember to have fun and be yourself!

[!] **Read the introduction section 'Building and Marketing Your Business'**
See page 12 of your *Connecting Mum Entrepreneurs* book for the complete text about this topic.

---

3 EASY STEPS TO ANSWER THAT FEARFUL QUESTION...
'WHAT DO YOU DO?'

Sometime's it can be hard to explain in a few words the whole idea behind your business and the essence of what you're offering. Despite this, you can't avoid the question. It will keep coming back when you participate in events and come across new opportunities. The following exercise will help you build your confidence when you meet new people and it's time to introduce yourself.

Example of an answer:

'*Typically I work with* international speakers with training programs to sell, *who have the challenge of* plateaued business growth and reduced profits.'

'*What I do is* secure JV partners to fill their events with prequalified leads, increasing their conversion rate and profitability.'

STEP 1: Your Ideal Customer. Who are they? Add a few key specifics.
Finish the statement statement by writing in your own ideal client.
Example: 'Typically I work with *international speakers with training programs to sell.*'

Typically I work with ....

....

....

....

....

....

....

....

STEP 2: Their Challenges You Solve:
Example: 'Who have the challenge of *plateaued business growth and reduced profits*.'

Who have the challenge of... ....

....

....

....

....

....

STEP 3: Results/Outcomes for the Clients:
Example: 'What I do is *secure JV partners to fill their events with prequalified leads, increasing their conversion rate and profitability*.'

By helping them do/achieve... ('What I do is...') ....

....

....

....

....

....

YOUR NEXT STEPS:
The following mission is then to go forth Courageously Confident and accept all challenges of 'What do you do?' with grace. Practise, Practise, Practise — In front on the mirror, in the car, in the shower every day for a month.

WHAT IS *Connecting?*

LIVING AN EXTRAORDINARILY CONNECTED LIFE

At a friendly BBQ, we are automatically relaxed and in a fun mood. There are no negative expectations or stories we tell ourselves, or thoughts about how others will react or what others may think of us. It is our perceptions of other people's potential reactions that make us feel uncomfortable in networking or connecting environments. At your next event, when you are meeting new people, simply lighten up and imagine yourself talking to your loved ones and your best friends.

> **!** **Read the section 'Living an Extraordinarily Connected Life'**
> See page 24 of your *Connecting Mum Entrepreneurs* book for the complete text about this topic.

What topics can help me add value to the conversation?

....

....

....

....

....

GIVE WITHOUT EXPECTATION

Having no expectations allows your mind to be open to any and all opportunities, no blinkers. Just have fun, ask questions, find out about others and let them talk about themselves. Have no expectations. You will be remembered as someone from the event that cared about them and wanted to know about *them*.

> **!** **Read the section 'The 4 Laws of Connecting'**
> See page 26 of your *Connecting Mum Entrepreneurs* book for the complete text about this topic.

Write down 5 ways to add value to someone in your network with no strings attached:

1. ....
....

2. ....
....

3. ....
....

4. ....
....

5. ....
....

RECIPROCITY

The amount you get back is usually a lot more than what you give. So how do you deal with takers? Since you can't force reciprocity, when do you say enough is enough if the other person is not reciprocating?

We found it best to test and measure, if giving without expectation enhances the relationship and you know that the giving is mutual then <u>we keep going</u>. If it is a draining process and all the other person does is take, <u>we stop</u> and usually move on from the relationship.

At an event, when you are meeting other mums in business, you have so many opportunities available to you. If someone is being a taker and not giving back what you are giving them after a certain period of time, politely excuse yourself and simply move on and entertain someone else.

> **!** **Read the section 'The 4 Laws of Connecting'**
> See page 26 of your *Connecting Mum Entrepreneurs* book for the complete text about this topic.

Write down 3 ways to excuse yourself from a taker / energy drainer / inspiration vampire (the 'OMG leave me alone' person.)

1. ....

....

2. ....

....

3. ....

....

LOVE AND PASSIONS

Speak from the heart. You will stick out like a sore thumb and your attitude will be deeply appreciated. When you do this you are not selling, you are simply sharing what you are passionate about and letting others decide if it resonates with them as well.

> **!** **Read the section 'The 4 Laws of Connecting'**
> See page 34 of your *Connecting Mum Entrepreneurs* book for the complete text about this topic.

What are my passions?

....

....

....

....

....

....

....

....

....

....

....

....

....

....

THE STORY BEHIND THE SALES STORY

The first step to working with someone is understanding their essence. This means that if their passions are congruent with what they are doing and those two visibly and energetically match, then there is a possibility of working together, whether they are a customer, a partner or an alliance.

> **[!]** **Read the sections 'The Essence of People'**
> **and 'The Story Behind the Sales Story'**
> See pages 17 & 35 of your *Connecting Mum Entrepreneurs* book for the complete text about this topic.

What is your story behind your sales story?

....

....

....

....

....

....

....

....

....

....

....

....

What is your 'WHY?'

My 'WHY' is ....

....

....

....

....

....

What is the reason you do what you do, aside from money?

❏ Freedom

❏ Flexible schedule

❏ Self expression

❏ Old dream or hobby

❏ Help others

❏ Need for a change of career

❏ Health reasons

❏ Adventure

❏ Innovative ideas

❏ Discover new passions

I want to ....

....

....

....

....

....

MAPPING OUT *your Connections*

STARTING BLOCKS TO YOUR CONNECTION MAP

Over and over again, it becomes clear that people take two things for granted:
Who they have at their fingertips and what these people are great at

> **!** **Read the section 'Starting Blocks to Your Connection Map'**
> See page 41 of your *Connecting Mum Entrepreneurs* book for the complete text about this topic.

Name at least 5 people who are close to you and what they're great at.

WHO: → IS GREAT AT:

1. ....

2. ....

3. ....

4. ....

5. ....

6. ....

7. ....

8. ....

9. ....

TAKE A SNAPSHOT OF YOUR NETWORK

Before you start mapping out your network on paper, think about whom you know. It's easiest to imagine this process in a series of concentric circles. Start with your immediate family, your partner's family, your children's friends, their parents, the school your children attend, your friends and so on. Just imagine all the people you must know, directly or indirectly.

> **!** **Read the section 'Take a Snapshot of Your Network'**
> See page 52 of your *Connecting Mum Entrepreneurs* book for the complete text about this topic.

1) **How many people do you know at the moment? Take a quick guess!**

   ....

2) **How do you go about generating business at the moment? Networking, Direct Mail, Email Marketing, etc.?**

   ....
   ....
   ....
   ....
   ....
   ....

3) **How often do you keep in touch with your connections, customers and members of your databases? Daily, weekly, monthly, annually, etc.?**

   ....

4) How much do you spend monthly on generating leads and new business-growth opportunities?

$ ....

5) When you go to a networking event and receive a business card from someone, what do you do with it? What happens after the event?

....

....

....

....

....

6) Out of every 10 customers, how many on average originate from your network?

....

7) When you think of the people you know (i.e. the people in you network) do you pre-judge them by saying 'they wouldn't buy from me/help me'?

❏ Yes   ❏ No

WHY? ....

....

....

....

....

....

SEGMENT YOUR LIFE

It can be difficult to just begin writing down hundreds, or even thousands of names with no plan! Just like Rory did with his Network, he first wrote down the different aspects of his life. It is time for you to do the same.

In the following columns, write down the different areas of your life. It could be based on friends, family, workplace, children's friends, schools, partner's friends, family, etc.:

> **[!] Read the section 'Segment Your Life'**
> See page 53 of your *Connecting Mum Entrepreneurs* book for the complete text about this topic.

Great! You now have the basis for your Connection Map. These different areas of your life will form the branches that sprout out from your central node.

Use the central node (circle in the middle of the page) and come up with a name for your network. If you are feeling a bit unimaginative, then you might want to call it 'My Network', 'The Connected Business Mum' or for the more creatively inclined 'It's not what you know, it's who you know!'

Put the name you choose into the central point.

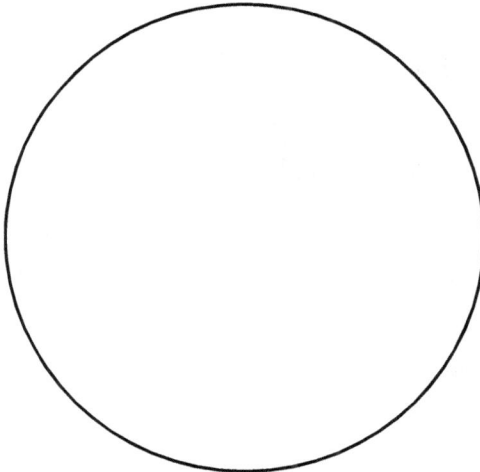

MIND MAP QUESTIONS

To give you a head start we have included a whole bunch of questions that should get the creative juices flowing. Remember not to pre-judge anyone! Repeat this process with all the different segments you listed out on the previous page. One by one, go around and write down as many names as you can within each segment.

> **[!] Read the chapter 'Mapping Out Your Connections'**
> See page 39 of your *Connecting Mum Entrepreneurs* book for the complete text about this topic.

1. Country I was born in:

a) Who are my relatives where I was born?

b) Who do I receive Christmas cards and letters from overseas?

c) My workplace: Do they have an international presence? Who do I know in that international arena?

d) Who do I speak to on Facebook regularly?

....

....

....

....

....

....

....

....

....

e) Who sent me an invitation recently?

....

....

....

....

....

....

....

....

f) Who has an upcoming birthday, engagement, wedding or other special day?

....

....

....

....

....

....

....

....

2. Country I now live in:

a) Who are my friends where I now live?

....

....

....

....

....

....

....

....

b) Who are my relatives where I live now?

....

....

....

....

....

....

....

....

....

....

c) Who do I get Christmas cards, letters, postcards or E-cards from?

....

....

....

....

....

....

....

....

....

....

d) Who are my top 10 closest friends?

....

....

....

....

....

e) Who do I go on holidays with?

f) Who do I know interstate?

....

....

....

....

....

....

....

....

....

g) Who do I know really well in business that is interstate?

....

....

....

....

....

....

....

....

....

h) Who are my 'once in a blue moon' contacts?

....
....
....
....
....
....

 ## 3. Employment:

a) How many companies have I worked for? Who are the people I know at each company?

....
....
....
....
....
....
....
....
....
....

b) Who do I work with now?

....

....

....

....

....

....

c) Who are all the people I know at work?

....

....

....

....

....

....

....

....

....

....

....

....

....

d) Who do I know in associations and unions I am a member of?

....

....

....

....

....

....

....

....

....

....

e) Am I a member of a social club? Who do I know there?

....

....

....

....

....

....

....

....

....

f) Am I an SME (subject matter expert) at work? Who turns to me for help?

....

....

....

....

....

....

....

....

....

g) Who do I see in the lift, car park, train or bus on the way to work?

....

....

....

....

....

....

....

....

....

♡ 4. Family tree:

a) Who is in my immediate family? Brothers, sisters, parents?

....

....

....

....

....

....

....

....

b) How many in-laws have I had?

....

....

....

....

....

....

....

....

c) Who are my aunties, uncles, cousins, second cousins and whom are they
    married to?

....

....

....

....

....

....

....

....

....

....

....

....

....

....

....

....

....

....

....

5. Hobbies:

a) What hobbies have I had? Who have I known within each hobby I have had?

....
....
....
....
....
....
....
....
....

b) What hobbies have my kids and partner(s) had?

....
....
....
....
....
....
....
....

c) What groups are associated with my hobbies?

....

....

....

....

....

....

....

....

d) How do my groups/hobbyists communicate with each other?
    Who do I communicate with?

....

....

....

....

....

....

....

....

....

e) Is my hobby nationally or globally popular? Who do I know within these areas or who can introduce me to these areas?

....

....

....

....

....

....

....

6. Neighbours:

a) How many addresses have I had? Who did I live next to at each address?

....

....

....

....

....

....

....

....

b) How many people were there at each of theses addresses?

....

....

....

....

....

....

....

....

....

....

7. Own business:

a) Who were/are my suppliers?

....

....

....

....

....

....

....

....

b) Who were/are my clients?

c) Who were/are my distributors?

....

....

....

....

....

....

....

....

....

....

d) Who were/are the reps that see me?

....

....

....

....

....

....

....

....

....

....

e) Who did I advertise with?

f) Who were/are my staff members?

g) Who were/are my service providers?

....

....

....

....

....

....

....

....

....

h) Have I had previous businesses? Who were my employees, clients, suppliers?

....

....

....

....

....

....

....

....

i) Who are the people whose business cards are most likely in a pile in my office somewhere?

....

....

....

8. Our kids' contacts:

When you are writing down your kids' contacts, it is not about whom your kids talk to, but whom you talk to while you are in your kids' environment. (e.g. who do you speak to when you are watching your son play sport?) Refer to Rory's network for ideas.

a)   Who are my child's best friends and their family members? Who are their parents?

b) Who does my child speak to on Social Media? Who are their parents?

....
....
....
....
....
....
....
....
....

c) How many sports are my kids involved in (coaching, music, dance)?
   Who are the parents in each of these activities?

....
....
....
....
....
....
....
....
....
....

9. Schooling:

a) Where did I go to school and who was in my class?

b) Who do I still see from kindergarten, primary- and secondary school?

....
....
....
....
....
....
....
....

c) Who do I/did I know at TAFE or University?

....
....
....
....
....
....
....
....
....
....
....

d) While at school, who impacted me the most? (These can be great teachers as well.)

....
....
....
....
....
....
....
....
....
....
....
....

10. Service Providers:

a) Who cuts my hair?

....
....
....
....

b) Who makes my lunch everyday?

....

....

....

....

c) Who do I buy my cappuccinos from?

....

....

....

....

d) What trades or maintenance do I use?

....

....

....

....

....

....

....

....

....

e) Girls: who makes me look beautiful? (Waxing, chiropractor, massage.)

f) Where do I catch up with my friends?

@ **11. Social Media Networks:**

a) What Social Media do I use? Who are my friends on Social Media?

b) What groups or pages am I a member of? Who is also a fan of those groups and pages?

....

....

....

....

....

....

....

....

....

c) Who do I communicate with regularly?

....

....

....

....

....

....

....

....

....

....

12. Sport:

a) What sports do I do? Who are the people in them?

....

....

....

....

....

....

....

....

....

....

b) Who did I hang around the playground with, as a kid?

....

....

....

....

....

....

c) What sports have I played and who were (are) my teammates?

d) Who was my favourite coach?

e) What was my favourite activity as a kid? Who did I play with?

....

....

....

....

....

....

....

....

....

....

f) Who do I know that is big into sports?

....

....

....

....

....

....

....

....

....

....

13. Your mobile contacts:

a) Who is in my mobile phone?

b) Who is in my email contact list?

....

....

....

....

....

....

....

....

....

....

....

....

....

....

....

....

....

....

....

....

c) Who do I receive a newsletter from?

_____ _____ _____

_____ _____ _____

_____ _____ _____

_____ _____ _____

_____ _____ _____

_____ _____ _____

_____ _____ _____

_____ _____ _____

_____ _____ _____

_____ _____ _____

_____ _____ _____

_____ _____ _____

_____ _____ _____

_____ _____ _____

Once you have finished, count up all the people on your list:

I have _____ connections.

DETERMINE THE QUALITY OF YOUR CONNECTIONS

So far you have written down everyone you know, without taking into account how well you know them. It's time to find out how strong your current connections are.

! **Read the section 'Determine the Quality of Your Connections'**
See page 59 of your *Connecting Mum Entrepreneurs* book for the complete text about this topic.

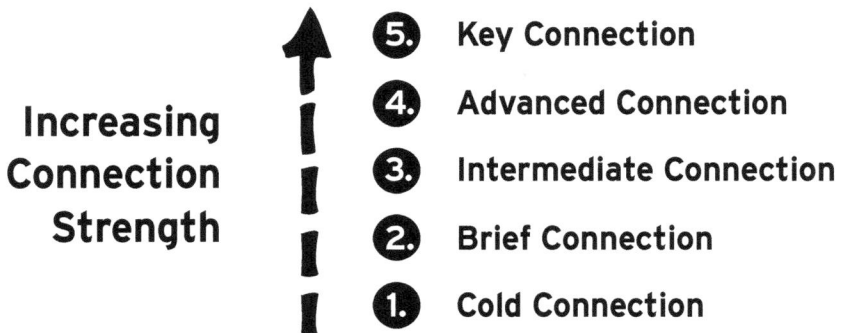

Increasing Connection Strength ↑

5. Key Connection

4. Advanced Connection

3. Intermediate Connection

2. Brief Connection

1. Cold Connection

There are 5 stages of connections. These 5 stages make up the flow of a relationship from first meeting to becoming a key part of your life.

DEFINITIONS

5. Key Connection: This is what you are aiming for. You know them and they know you nearly inside out. These are the people who turn to you and who you turn to when help is needed. It might be in a business, financially or anything personal as well. These are the people who you would go out of your way for and vice versa, that is how strong the rapport is. At this stage you can move forward together and blitz anything and everything life throws at you! These are the people that often become mentors and trusted allies.

4. Advanced Connection: You know this person really well. They are usually great friends with a very high level of rapport. If you are having a party, a BBQ or drinks, they are on the invite list. You don't have to have known them for long, but you do have to know them well and feel really comfortable with them. You would characterise these people as best friends

3. Intermediate Connection: This is the stage everyone is familiar with. It is the stage where you call people 'friends'. You are comfortable with these people, you know them quite well. You know what they do, why they do it, and what their passions are.

2. Brief Connection: You may have seen these people a few times here and there, but you don't know much about them. You may know roughly what they do and who they are, but haven't really had the opportunity to properly connect. You might find them interesting and would like to know out more about them.

1. Cold Connection: Someone you have never met. You know nothing about them and vice versa. If you don't know how to add value to what they do then they are usually a cold connection.

Look back at your Connection Map and find the people that fit into the *Key Connection* (#5) and *Advanced Connection* (#4) areas.

Mark their names by either putting a 5 or a 4 next to them, or highlighting them in some way that makes sense to you.

FOR EXAMPLE:

Ryan	Bob C.	Mary
Sally	Arel	Suzy ④
Mark ⑤	Helen	Lisa

STRATEGIC NETWORKING

Most people build their network in a chaotic way with no definition, no strategy and without key people of influence; it's an absolute clutter. This is called an *'accidental network'*. Although this type of network may look full of potential at first as it contains many people, none of the participants can truly help you add value to your business or expand your network further to find new opportunities. An accidental network might bring you accidental success, but also little control on how much energy you will end up spending trying to expand it.

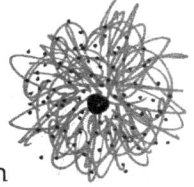

Your wealth network only requires you to create relationships with a small group of KEY people that you share core values with. They are active participants in your life and business, not spectators. Instead of building an *accidental network*, you can invest your time and energy in building a *strategic wealth network* that will be composed of key people that can help you grow. Not only clients or customers but a network of people who know, like, respect and trust you.

In a *Strategic Wealth Network Pyramid*, there are 3 clusters. Within each cluster, connections within your network have different roles. Roles are assigned to people based on your relationship with them, their personality, congruency, gifts, experience and wisdom.

Poverty Network

TAKERS	Those that when they ring, your mind says, 'Oh God, what do they want now?'
DOUBTERS	'I don't know why I bother telling them anything, they always knock me down.'
PASSENGERS	It's nice to see them but there is no forward movement, no contribution in ideas, conversation or growth. The 'hang out' and 'hang around' crowd. 'God, I feel tired now, are they draining my energy and motivation?'
DISTRACTORS	They come around when you are in activity and distract you. The 'don't go home yet, stay a little longer' group. Always willing to pull you off track to further their own self interest. 'Damn it, the time has just vanished today, what happened?'

Supportive Network

SUPPORTERS   They make you feel great, buff you up. When you think of them, you smile.

PEERS   They are like you and you are supportive of each other.

CONNECTORS   Suggest people you should connect with.

CHEER LEADERS   Tell others how great you are, but may not be specific. 'Oh God, what do they want now?'

Wealth Network

ELDERS   Have industry or specialised knowledge, mentors.

SCOUTS AND OPPORTUNISTS   They know all the latest, newest opportunities and information, are abreast of changes in the market place. Their knowledge may be generic in the early stages until they niche into a specific area.

WHEELERS AND DEALERS   Always make money on the deal, focus is on them, but they are great to have as a negotiators on your team.

LEADERS   Have the natural gift of leadership, where people naturally follow and listen to them.

MANAGERS   Great at organisations, managing and will run things better than you can.

INTRODUCERS AND CONNECTORS   Actually make the introduction to the other parties for you. Better quality, higher level connectors, they instigate connections and introductions.

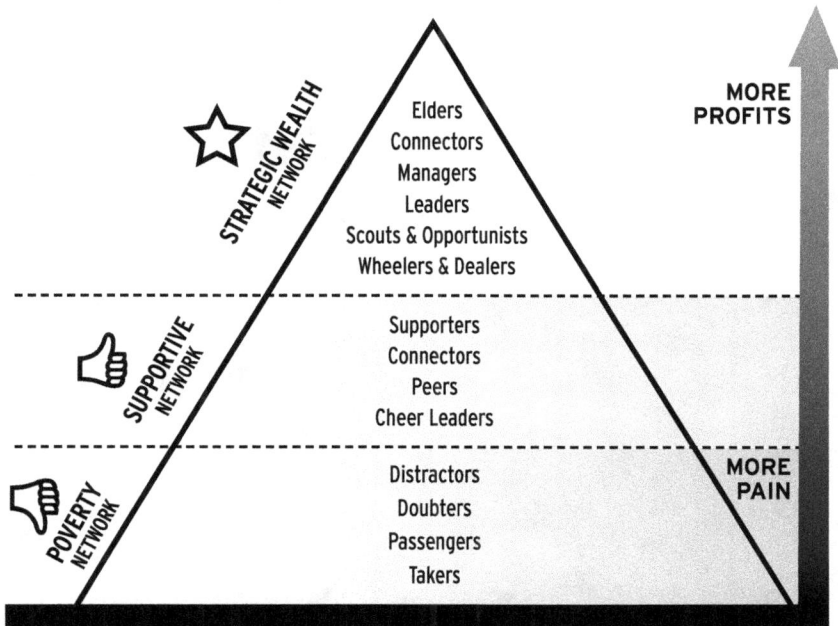

STRATEGIC WEALTH NETWORK
Elders
Connectors
Managers
Leaders
Scouts & Opportunists
Wheelers & Dealers

SUPPORTIVE NETWORK
Supporters
Connectors
Peers
Cheer Leaders

POVERTY NETWORK
Distractors
Doubters
Passengers
Takers

MORE PROFITS

MORE PAIN

People who are content with where they are would most likely consider the TOP successful people as the ones they know the best, the ones that are within their comfort zone. The problem with this approach is that you will continue to stay where you are at, not moving forward and not moving upward very quickly. The higher the quality of people in your network, the better it can help you perform. When you choose the people in your network rationally, those who are exceptional will stand out and you will start to take notice of who they lead to, where they network and who their friends are. This opens up new spheres of influence to you and can lead you to other participants for you to add to your strategic network.

From the lists you just filled out in the previous pages, write down the TOP 5 people who have the most influence and how you identify them.

WHO HAS THE MOST INFLUENCE → HOW YOU IDENTIFY WITH THAT PERSON

1.

2.

3.

4.

5.

WHO HAS SPECIALISED KNOWLEDGE? → HOW YOU IDENTIFY WITH THAT PERSON

1. ....

2. ....

3. ....

4. ....

5. ....

WHO HAS THE MOST EXPERIENCE IN → HOW YOU IDENTIFY WITH THAT PERSON
YOUR FIELD OR THE FIELD YOU ARE
WANTING TO EXPLORE?

1. ....

2. ....

3. ....

4. ....

5. ....

WHO IS THE MOST SUPPORTIVE? → HOW YOU IDENTIFY WITH THAT PERSON

1. ....

2. ....

3. ....

4. ....

5. ....

WHO ARE THE PEOPLE THAT → HOW YOU IDENTIFY WITH THAT PERSON
SEEM TO KNOW EVERYONE AND
THE NATURAL STORY TELLERS?

1. ....

2. ....

3. ....

4. ....

5. ....

**WHO ARE THE PEOPLE THAT HOLD
YOU BACK?** → **HOW YOU IDENTIFY WITH THAT PERSON**

1. ....

2. ....

3. ....

4. ....

5. ....

**WHO ARE THE PEOPLE IN YOUR
BUSINESS THAT DOUBT WHAT YOU
ARE DOING WITH NO FOUNDATION
FOR THEIR CLAIMS?** → **HOW YOU IDENTIFY WITH THAT PERSON**

1. ....

2. ....

3. ....

4. ....

5. ....

WHO ARE THE PEOPLE IN YOUR LIFE THAT ALWAYS SEEM TO TAKE BUT NEVER GIVE? → HOW YOU IDENTIFY WITH THAT PERSON

1. ....

2. ....

3. ....

4. ....

5. ....

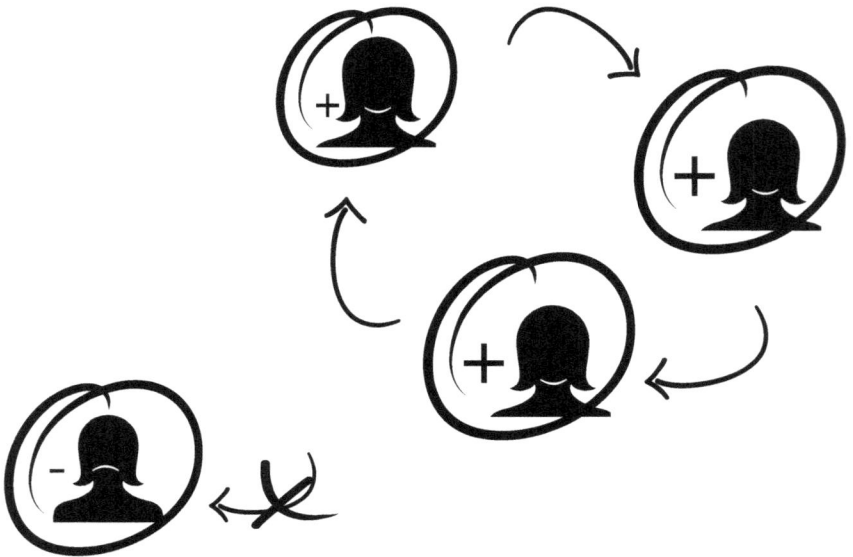

For this stage we want to identify the people that are actually participating in your life and business. These people don't have to actually speak to you personally, they just need to have an influence on your life in some way. Some people will have greater interactions than others but everyone in your Strategic Wealth Network must be a participant, <u>no spectators allowed</u>. Once you have identified your real participants, you are ready to fill in your Strategic Wealth Network Pyramid by assigning roles to people.

Who are the people that you identified in the previous section that:

⭐ **Have an active influence in contributing to your <u>wealth</u> in your life?**

....

....

....

....

....

....

....

....

👍 **Have an active influence in <u>supporting</u> you and your business?**

....

....

....

....

....

....

....

👎 **Have an active influence in <u>keeping you poor</u>?**
It can be poor business growth, management or building wealth.

....

....

....

....

....

....

....

Going back to the lists on the previous pages, identify the people in your Sphere of Influence that fit into the following Roles within each of the 3 Clusters.

You don't have to fill in every spot. Most people will have gaps that need to be filled. The following sections cover exactly how to fill those with the best people possible, so don't worry if you have some gaps in your Strategic Wealth Network.

☆ WEALTH NETWORK	First Choice	Second Choice
Elders		
Connectors		
Managers		
Leaders		
Scouts and Opportunists		
Wheelers and Dealers		

👍 SUPPORTIVE NETWORK	First Choice	Second Choice
Supporters		
Connectors		
Peers		
Cheer Leaders		

👎 POVERTY NETWORK	First Choice	Second Choice
Distractors		
Doubters		
Passengers		
Takers		

Now Complete Your Strategic Wealth Network Pyramid below:

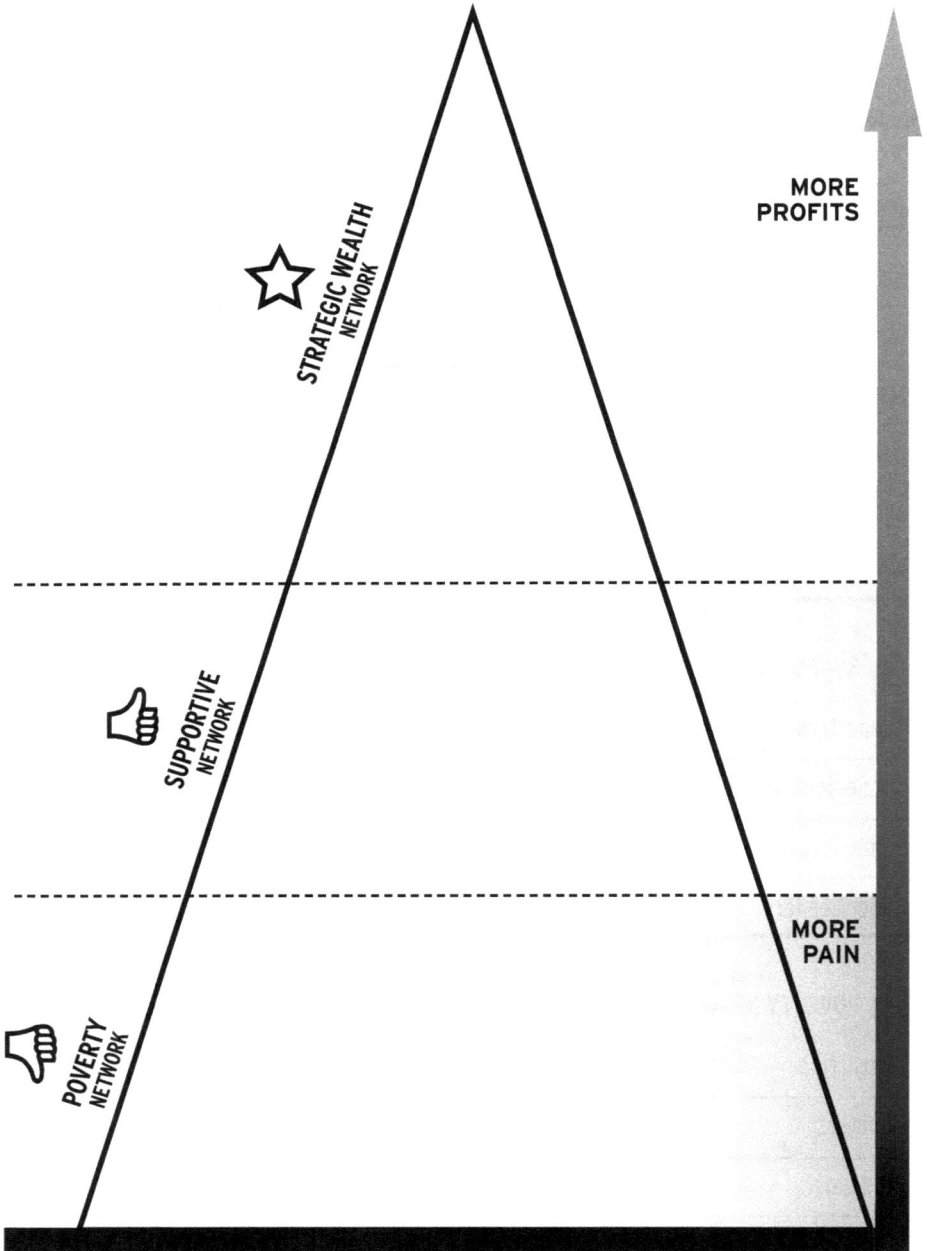

STRATEGIC WEALTH NETWORK

SUPPORTIVE NETWORK

POVERTY NETWORK

MORE PROFITS

MORE PAIN

LEVERAGE POINT

Think about a specific goal or outcome you have for your business.

The way you reach that goal or outcome faster is by identifying commonalities with people in your network, that have the ability to help you, but preferably help each other.

The way to find these similarities is by asking questions about some of the intermediate, advanced and key connections in your network.

Questions like:
› Who do they know?
› Where do they have influence?
› What industries do they associate with, have worked in or have links to?
› What do they love doing and is it relevant to what you are trying to achieve?
› What hobbies, sports or schools are they involved with?
› What states or countries have they worked in?
› What special skills, expertise or natural talents do they have?

! **Read the section 'Leverage Points and Circles of Influence'**
See page 63 of your *Connecting Mum Entrepreneurs* book for the complete text about this topic.

After looking at your Strategic Wealth Network and the participants within it, who is missing? Describe them or the skills you are looking for.

1-AWAY CONNECTIONS

Now you have an understanding of leverage points and circles of influence you are ready for the *1-Aways*... this is where you raise your understanding to where you are only ever one connection away from the one you need or want. As you look back to your Connection Map, you will no doubt start to see the enormous amount of potential right in front of you. This gets taken to a higher level in the *1-Aways*.

If you look at your map, each person you wrote down also has a network. These *1-Aways* are a gold mine for expanding your network, as you know someone with whom you have rapport, who has a direct link to that *1-Away* connection.

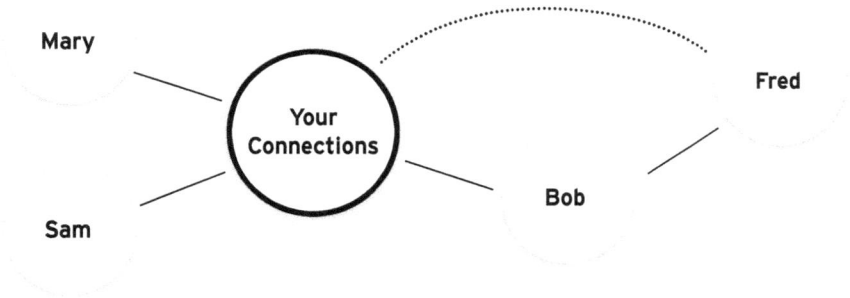

Read the section '*1-Away* Connections'
See page 66 of your *Connecting Mum Entrepreneurs* book for the complete text about this topic.

Who can help you get to that *1-Away* connection and what action steps can you take to get in touch with people who got the skills you need to add to your network? Jot your thoughts and action steps down here so you can easily refer back to them.

Skill needed:

....

Who can help me in my network: Who is the *1-Away* connection:

....   >   ....

ACTION STEP to connect with the *1-Away* connection:

....

....

....

....

Action step will be completed before this date: _____   Check (✓) this box when completed [   ]

Skill needed:

....

Who can help me in my network: Who is the *1-Away* connection:

....   >   ....

ACTION STEP to connect with the *1-Away* connection:

....

....

....

....

Action step will be completed before this date: _____   Check (✓) this box when completed [   ]

Skill needed:

....

Who can help me in my network: Who is the *1-Away* connection:

.... ⟩ ....

ACTION STEP to connect with the *1-Away* connection:

....

....

....

....

Action step will be completed before this date: Check (✓)
                                                        this box when
                                                        completed

---

Skill needed:

....

Who can help me in my network: Who is the *1-Away* connection:

.... ⟩ ....

ACTION STEP to connect with the *1-Away* connection:

....

....

....

....

Action step will be completed before this date: Check (✓)
                                                        this box when
                                                        completed

Skill needed:

....

Who can help me in my network: Who is the *1-Away* connection:

.... >   ....

ACTION STEP to connect with the *1-Away* connection:

....

....

....

....

Action step will be completed before this date: [   ]   Check (✓) this box when completed [   ]

Skill needed:

....

Who can help me in my network: Who is the *1-Away* connection:

.... >   ....

ACTION STEP to connect with the *1-Away* connection:

....

....

....

....

Action step will be completed before this date: [   ]   Check (✓) this box when completed [   ]

Skill needed:

....

Who can help me in my network: Who is the *1-Away* connection:

....

ACTION STEP to connect with the *1-Away* connection:

....

....

....

....

Action step will be completed before this date: Check (✓)
this box when
completed

Skill needed:

....

Who can help me in my network: Who is the *1-Away* connection:

....

ACTION STEP to connect with the *1-Away* connection:

....

....

....

....

Action step will be completed before this date: Check (✓)
this box when
completed

Skill needed:

....

Who can help me in my network: Who is the *1-Away* connection:

.... > ....

ACTION STEP to connect with the *1-Away* connection:

....

....

....

....

Action step will be completed before this date: Check (✓)
                                                          this box when
                                                          completed

---

Skill needed:

....

Who can help me in my network: Who is the *1-Away* connection:

.... > ....

ACTION STEP to connect with the *1-Away* connection:

....

....

....

....

Action step will be completed before this date: Check (✓)
                                                          this box when
                                                          completed

Skill needed:

....

Who can help me in my network: Who is the *1-Away* connection:

.... > ....

ACTION STEP to connect with the *1-Away* connection:

....

....

....

....

Action step will be completed before this date: _____

Check (✓) this box when completed ____

Skill needed:

....

Who can help me in my network: Who is the *1-Away* connection:

.... > ....

ACTION STEP to connect with the *1-Away* connection:

....

....

....

....

Action step will be completed before this date: _____

Check (✓) this box when completed ____

Skill needed:

....

Who can help me in my network: Who is the *1-Away* connection:

.... > ....

ACTION STEP to connect with the *1-Away* connection:

....

....

....

....

Action step will be completed before this date: | Check (✓) this box when completed

---

Skill needed:

....

Who can help me in my network: Who is the *1-Away* connection:

.... > ....

ACTION STEP to connect with the *1-Away* connection:

....

....

....

....

Action step will be completed before this date: | Check (✓) this box when completed

Skill needed:

Who can help me in my network: Who is the *1-Away* connection:

ACTION STEP to connect with the *1-Away* connection:

Action step will be completed before this date: Check (✓) this box when completed

---

Skill needed:

Who can help me in my network: Who is the *1-Away* connection:

ACTION STEP to connect with the *1-Away* connection:

Action step will be completed before this date: Check (✓) this box when completed

Skill needed:

....

Who can help me in my network: Who is the *1-Away* connection:

....

ACTION STEP to connect with the *1-Away* connection:

....

....

....

....

Action step will be completed before this date: Check (✓)
this box when
completed

Skill needed:

....

Who can help me in my network: Who is the *1-Away* connection:

....

ACTION STEP to connect with the *1-Away* connection:

....

....

....

....

Action step will be completed before this date: Check (✓)
this box when
completed

Skill needed:

....

Who can help me in my network: Who is the *1-Away* connection:

....   >   ....

ACTION STEP to connect with the *1-Away* connection:

....

....

....

....

Action step will be completed before this date: Check (✓)
this box when
completed

Skill needed:

....

Who can help me in my network: Who is the *1-Away* connection:

....   >   ....

ACTION STEP to connect with the *1-Away* connection:

....

....

....

....

Action step will be completed before this date: Check (✓)
this box when
completed

NETWORK *Directory*

Now that you have a completed connection map, it's time to collect their contact details, if you don't already have them.

Spend some time organising them by industry type, name, and job title or put them in the order of how they appear on your connection map (however your prefer really).

Or use one of the many apps that you can get for your smart phone to do this for you if that is your preference.

> **!** **Read the section 'Keeping Track and In Touch'**
> See page 68 of your *Connecting Mum Entrepreneurs* book for the complete text about this topic.

THE *Wow* FACTOR

PURPOSE AND PASSION DISCOVERY

It is so much more fun and impacting to add value and be connected. Putting yourself in a position to play more together, share and empower others, creating a ripple effect with great stories that make people think differently, cause paradigm shifts and change things for the better.

Okay, but what if the little voice in your head is saying, 'Yeah, but I don't feel comfortable using that approach or that doesn't suit my personality.'

Then the distinction that I would like to make here is that it's not about you becoming someone different or using different words, it's about exploring other options that work really well for you.

> **[!] Read the section 'Purpose and Passion Discovery'**
> See page 88 of your *Connecting Mum Entrepreneurs* book for the complete text about this topic.

Try this scenario by answering the following questions to see how you can express your purpose and passions.
You may try this exercise many times to see what is the best scenario for you.

What do you want most out of life?
Write 2 different answers.

A1) ....

....

A2) ....

....

What do you want for this planet?
Write 2 different answers.

B1) ....

....

B2) ....

....

What makes you special?
Write 2 different answers.

C1) ....

....

C2) ....

....

What can you do today?
Write 2 different answers.

D1) ....

....

D2) ....

....

Now place your answers in the blank spaces below:

I will (D1) ....

using my (C1) ....

to achieve (B1) ....

so will achieve (A1) ....

You may need to round out the edges in each scenario so it makes complete sense. The magic in this exercise is that the results are hidden until the end so your brain cannot jump ahead and figure out the answer you think it should be.

In our experience, most people that express what they do by relating it back to their above answers have a radical change in their body language, facial expressions and energy. Before it seemed like 'going through the motions', whereas afterwards it feels like a heartfelt response, full of enthusiasm and excitement, highlighting that this person has a true passion for what they do.

YOUR OWN UNIQUENESS

Allowing your *Uniqueness* or your *Giftedness* to run wild is where you will be most in flow, where things are the easiest and you can be 100% totally unashamedly yourself.

Your 'Why' and your Uniqueness/Giftedness help you go from the hesitant and unconfident kid on the left to the ecstatic and excited kid on the right:

True connections are created by the essence of people
and your own uniqueness

[!] Read the section 'Your Own Uniqueness'
See page 88 of your *Connecting Mum Entrepreneurs* book for the complete text about this topic.

What are the things that make you unique?
They could be quirks or specific skill sets that you have. If you get stuck, ask your partner or a Key Connection.

....

....

....

....

....

....

What can you do start using your uniqueness in your business/career if you don't already, or what can you do to leverage your uniqueness even more than what you are already doing?

ABOUT THE AUTHOR

Sally A Curtis helps overwhelmed, frustrated mums in business.
For heaps of FREE resources check out her website
www.BusinessMumsSolutions.com
Sharing is Sally's way to HELP mums just like her.

Sally has built **Business Mums Solutions** from the ground up, where you will find heaps of information on building great businesses, growing great kids and saving time, so you have 'me' time, as well. Sally has shared a lot of great information in this book for mums in business and continues to share tools and resources on her blog, website, social media sites, seminars and live trainings.

Sally exists to share as much of her wisdom, skills, tools and stories as she can to help mums in business. She is all about simplicity (Sally loves all things Apple) and saving time is her strongest driver. If Sally can share a tool or resources that gives you more time to spend with your family; or a new strategy to grow your business more effectively, then her heart will sing.

If she can inspire you with stories on how to enrol your kids in your business and vision; or inspire you to keep going, then she has achieved one of her greatest goals.

If you're out of the start-up phase then Sally will help you with the next fastest way to grow through simple Joint Ventures. She will use her skills to help you so don't hesitate to contact Sally today.

Sally has started several of her own businesses from scratch, because 'they sounded like a good idea at the time'. She has poured her heart into business: her blood, sweat, tears and tantrums... and made each business work. She has done this with an 18-month old who is now 12. She had fun along the way.

Sally is also a keen investor. Through her eyes she looks at business and people as an investment in our futures. Sally is an advocate of making mutual decisions, keeping an eye on the numbers, making it happen, and growing great kids by leading by example.

Sally's two most favourite quotes are:
> *'When the student is ready, the teacher will appear.'*
> *'Opportunities are a daily occurrence and often hidden in plain sight.'*

Sally has over 20 years of business development experience across a variety of industries ranging from cosmetics, to retail, media and events and franchising.

She has worked for well-known companies including: Aussie Farmers Direct, Val Morgan, McCain Foods and Clinique, plus alongside many outstanding entrepreneurs. Sally has always contributed to the growth of organisations through developing new business, leveraging existing relationships and implementing strategic initiatives. She loves to see business and growth made simple.

Sally has spent a number of years as a consultant to various global events organisations, ensuring that the events are well attended and run effectively, making significant profit margins.

Some of Sally's previous clients include:

Dale Beaumont - CEO of Dream Express International Pty Ltd

Duane Alley - Founder and CEO of Performance Results Pty Ltd

Mike Handcock - Chairman and Founder of Rock Your Life Global

Dr Joanna Martin - Founder of One of Many and Shift Enterprises UK

Shaune Clarke - Founder of 6 Figure Speaker Training and Big Brand Speaking

NOTES

NOTES

www.ingramcontent.com/pod-product-compliance
Lightning Source LLC
Chambersburg PA
CBHW061609220326
41598CB00024BC/3509